Gifted & Talented

More Questions & Answers

For Ages 6–8

By Bailey Kennedy, M.S.

Illustrated by Larry Nolte

LOWELL HOUSE JUVENILE

LOS ANGELES

CONTEMPORARY BOOKS

CHICAGO

*To my family and close friends for their continued and
much appreciated love and support.*
— B.K.

Reviewed and endorsed by Joanne López, M.A.,
Veteran educator and member of the National Association for Gifted Children

ISBN: 1-56565-564-8

Library of Congress Catalog is available.

President and Publisher: Jack Artenstein
Director of Publishing Services: Rena Copperman
Managing Editor: Lindsey Hay
Editor in Chief, Juvenile: Amy Downing
Editor: Jessica Oifer
Art Director: Lisa-Theresa Lenthall

Lowell House books can be purchased at special discounts
when ordered in bulk for premiums and special sales.
Contact Department TC at the following address:
Lowell House Juvenile
2020 Avenue of the Stars, Suite 300
Los Angeles, CA 90067

Manufactured in the United States of America

10 9 8 7 6 5 4 3 2

Note to Parents

Teach a child facts and you give her knowledge. Teach her to think and you give her wisdom. This is the principle behind the entire series of Gifted and Talented® materials. And this is the reason that thinking skills are becoming stressed widely in classrooms throughout the country.

The questions and answers in the **Gifted & Talented® Question & Answer** books have been designed specifically to promote the development of critical and creative thinking skills. Each page features one "topic question" that is answered beneath a corresponding picture. This topic provides the springboard to the following questions on the page.

Each of the six related questions focuses on a different higher-level thinking skill. The skills include knowledge and recall, comprehension, deduction, inference, sequencing, prediction, classification, analyzing, problem solving, and creative expansion.

The topic question, answer, and artwork contain the answers or clues to the answers for some of the other questions. Certain questions, however, can only be answered by relating the topic to other facts that your child may know. In the back of the book are suggested answers to help you guide your child.

Effective questioning has been used to develop a child's intellectual gifts since the time of Socrates. Certainly, it is the most common teaching technique in classrooms today. But asking questions isn't as easy as it looks! Here are a few tips to keep in mind that will help you and your child use this book more effectively:

★ First of all, let your child flip through the book and select the questions and pictures that interest him or her. If the child wants to do only one page, that's great. If he or she only wants to answer some of the questions on a page, save the others for another time.

★ Unlike most books, this book does not have to be read consecutively. Each page is totally self-contained. Start at the back, the front, the middle—the choice is up to your child!

★ Give your child time to think! Pause at least 10 seconds before you offer any help. You'd be surprised how little time many parents and teachers give a child to think before jumping right in and answering a question themselves.

★ Help your child by restating or rephrasing the question if necessary. But again, make sure you pause and give the child time first. Also, don't ask the same question over and over! Go on to another question, or use hints to prompt your child when needed.

★ Encourage your child to give more details or expand answers by asking questions such as "What made you say that?" or "Why do you think so?"

★ This book will not only teach your child about many things, but it will teach you a lot about your child. Make the most of your time together—and have fun!

The answers in the back of the book are to be used as a guide. Sometimes your child may come up with an answer that is different but still a good answer. Remember, the principle behind all Gifted and Talented® materials is to **teach your child to think**—not just to give answers.

Who were the medieval knights?

Knights were men who fought in a king's army during the Middle Ages in Europe. The Middle Ages, also called the medieval times, lasted almost 1,000 years, from 476 A.D. to 1450 A.D. Boys trained for 13 years to become knights. They began their training at the age of 8. Knights had to know how to fight using a spear, called a *lance*, while on horseback. They wore protective armor that weighed over 60 pounds.

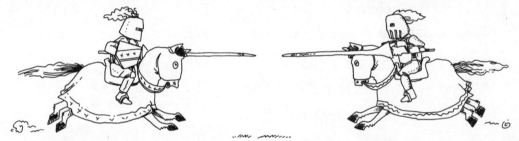

1. What could you do to find out more about knights?
2. If an 8-year-old boy was sent away for 13 years of training, how old would he be when he became a knight?
3. What stories have you heard or read about knights?
4. Create your own adventure story about a brave knight. What kind of adventures will he have?
5. What materials could you use to make a movable suit of armor to cover your entire body?
6. There were no televisions, lights, computers, or CDs during the Middle Ages. How would you entertain yourself without these things?

Why were castles first built?

Castles were first built around 5th century A.D. (during the Middle Ages) as fortresses to protect the lord, or king, his family, and his people. The very first castles were made of timber, or wood, and were surrounded by tall, strong wooden walls. Later, the castles were rebuilt with large stones to make them stronger. Thick stone walls with high towers for watchmen, or guards, were built around the castles.

1. Have you ever seen an actual castle or a ruin of a castle? Where was it? What did it look like? When was it first built?
2. Why were many castles built with a water-filled moat, or ditch, around them?
3. How do you think workmen in the Middle Ages were able to lift heavy stones and build large castles without modern equipment?
4. How could you create a castle from sand at the beach?
5. Design a castle of your own. Draw a picture of it on a separate piece of paper.
6. Make up a story about a king and queen, their family, and the castle workers who live in your castle drawing.

How do we use flags?

People have used flags for hundreds of years for many reasons. The symbol, seal, or pattern on a flag helps show the meaning of the flag. This design may stand for a country or a state or for an organization like the International Olympic Games Committee flag with its five interlinking rings. Flags are also used to send signals, messages, or warnings. The International Flag Code of Signals has a flag and a symbol for each letter of the alphabet so a message can be spelled out.

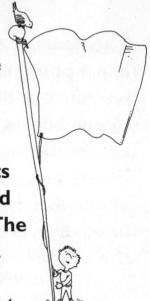

1. If you were having a birthday party at the beach, what flag signal would you use to tell friends where your party is?

2. Each state in the United States has its own flag. What is the symbol on your state's flag? What do you think it stands for?

3. Where could you find out about the International Flag Code of Signals? Which symbols would you use to spell your first name?

4. What is a color guard?

5. What does a person mean when he or she says "Flag down that car"?

6. Design a "me" flag that tells something about you. What colors and symbols will you use on your flag?

Why do our hearts beat faster when we run?

The heart is a strong muscle that is always working like a pump to move blood all around the body. When we run, our blood needs to get to the different parts of our bodies more quickly to provide more oxygen and keep them working properly. This makes our hearts beat, or pump the blood, faster. Our hearts are about the size of our fists. You can feel your heart beat, or pulse, by putting two fingers of one hand on the inside of the wrist on your other arm.

1. Can you think of any other times when your heart might beat faster?
2. Ask a friend if you can count his or her pulse. How would you do this? Does your friend's heartbeat feel faster or slower than yours?
3. If you wanted to use your ears to listen to your friend's heartbeat, where on your friend's body would you put your ear?

THUMP THUMP

4. What does a nurse or a doctor use to listen to your beating heart?

5. What does it mean when a person says "You are my heartthrob"?

6. What kind of a story can you create or make up about your beating heart? Write your story on a separate piece of paper.

One Step Further

Ask an adult to help you find your pulse and count the number of times it beats in 60 seconds. Count heartbeats when you are resting. Exercise for a few minutes by running, jumping rope, skipping, or hopping. Then count your pulse rate after this exercise. Was your heartbeat faster or slower after you exercised? Explain your answer.

What is a biography?

A biography is the story of one person's life as told by another person. Biographies are usually written about people who have worked hard to do special things in their lives, such as Harriet Tubman and Frederick Douglass. They both escaped from slavery and then helped other slaves to become free. A writer of biographies is called a *biographer*.

1. Where would you look for biographies of famous men and women?

2. What biographies have you read? Who was your favorite person to read about? What made him or her so special?

3. During what war were all the slaves in America freed?

4. Pretend you are a biographer who is going to write about a person living today. Who would you write about? Why?

5. A story that you write about yourself is called an *autobiography*. If you

were going to write your autobiography, what events in your life would be most interesting to your readers?

6. What illustrations would you include in your autobiography?

One Step Further

Ask an adult to help you create a timeline showing all the important events in your life. You may want to tape several pieces of paper together to make your timeline longer. Begin by drawing a long horizontal line. Put the date you were born at one end and today's date at the other end. Then divide your timeline into large equal sections, one section for every year you have lived. Now think about all the important things that have happened in your life. You might want to include events like when you first learned to walk and talk, when you started school, or when you learned to ride a bike. Put all of these special events in order according to how old you were when they happened. Write in the date on your timeline and draw a picture of your special event.

What types of stamps do people collect?

People enjoy collecting different types of postage stamps from various places in the world. Stamps that have already been used for postage and have been *canceled,* or marked by the post office, are often very valuable. Many people collect *commemorative* stamps, which are stamps that have been created to celebrate special events like the Olympic Games. Other people enjoy collecting stamps that have a common subject or theme in their design. Popular themes include flowers, birds, transportation, and famous people.

1. What is a canceled stamp? How does it get canceled?
2. Why does it cost less money for a postcard stamp than for an envelope stamp?
3. What kinds of commemorative stamps have you seen?
4. If you were to design a commemorative stamp, what special event would you show?
5. Look at the stamps on the mail delivered to your house. How many different designs do you see? What are they?
6. People put different stamps on a postcard, a letter, and a package. Why? How do people know what stamps to put on the different pieces of mail?

What kinds of people become explorers?

Explorers are very curious people who visit and study new and distant places. Throughout history, explorers have traveled to unknown lands in search of food, gold, and other treasures, as well as to trade for food and other goods they don't have. Today, explorers investigate what it is like under the oceans, on the tops of mountains, at the North and South Poles, and up in space.

1. What famous explorers have you heard about? What places did they explore and when?

2. How could you find out who first explored the moon? What did these explorers discover there?

3. Where would you most like to travel to and explore?

4. What would you have to do to become an explorer? What kind of special training or equipment would you need?

5. What does a surgeon do when he or she performs exploratory surgery?

6. Pretend you are a famous explorer writing in a daily journal about your latest explorations. What kinds of things would you record?

How is a truck different from a car?

A truck is built to carry all sorts of goods, called *cargo,* from one place to another. Trucks are bigger than cars, which are made to carry people. There are many different kinds of trucks. Some trucks carry the mail, and some haul lumber, oil, cars, or liquid such as gasoline. Large trucks that have two or more parts are called *rigs.* These trucks have a tractor, which is the front part, containing the engine and the cab where the driver sits. The second part of the truck is called the trailer, which holds the cargo. It is attached or hitched to the tractor. These large trucks are also called tractor-trailers.

1. How many different kinds of trucks have you seen? On a separate piece of paper, draw at least three different kinds of trucks.

2. You might hear a truck driver say "If you've got it, a truck brought it!" Look around your house. How many things do you see that were carried by a truck to the store where you and your family bought it?

3. What do you think a truck farmer does?

4. What is a hand truck? Why would people use one?

5. What would a person mean if he or she said "Just truck on down"?

6. Why do you think truck drivers are sometimes called "knights of the road"?

One Step Further

Some trucks have only 4 wheels, while others have as many as 18 wheels. For one week, keep a list of all the different kinds of trucks you see when you go out. How many wheels do each of these trucks have? Write down the kind of cargo you think the trucks are carrying. Look at the license plates and record the different states these trucks come from. How many trucks did you see altogether? What is the total number of wheels all of these trucks have?

What kinds of things can we measure?

We can measure many different types of things. We can measure the distance from one place to another, the speed a truck is traveling, the length of a strip of fabric, and the temperature at the North Pole. We can also measure the weight of a watermelon and the number of minutes it takes to get from home to school. Different measurement tools are used for taking each of these measurements.

1. Look at the pictures. What kinds of measurement tools are the people using?
2. What kind of tool would you use to find out how tall you are?
3. If someone says that you can play in the park for an hour and a half, how many minutes will it take for the time to pass?
4. What tools can you use to measure the passing of time?
5. What kinds of measurements were taken right after you were born? What tools did the nurse or the doctor use to take these measurements?
6. A baker uses a thermometer to measure the heat in the oven. Which professions can you name that use some sort of measurement tool?

How were things measured before there were rulers?

Many years ago, people used parts of their bodies to measure things. They measured the size of a field by counting how many steps it took to walk across it. They measured the height of a horse by counting the number of hand spans it was from top to bottom. (And we still do!) Because everyone had different-size hands, arms, and feet, and took different-size steps, their measurements were never the same.

1. How are the children in the pictures measuring the objects?
2. If you and an adult each used your own feet to measure the length of the same rug, would your measurements be the same or different? Why?
3. What parts of your body could you use to measure the size of your bedroom?
4. What parts of your body could you use to measure the height of your favorite toy, the width of your bathtub, or the length of your couch?
5. What other item(s) could you use to measure length?
6. Create a story about a village in which the citizens use different parts of their *own* bodies as measurement tools. What kinds of problems do they encounter?

What is the Great Wall of China?

The Great Wall of China is the longest structure ever built—1,500 miles long. It winds up and down the mountains of North China. Over 2,000 years ago, it was built to surround the city and protect the Chinese people from fierce barbarians who were attacking their villages. This huge wall joined together many older walls. The Great Wall of China was built to be as tall as five men and as wide as six horses at the top, and as wide as eight horses at the bottom. High watchtowers were built every 100 yards so

the barbarians could be seen coming. **Roadways on the top of the wall were wide enough for 10 soldiers to march side by side as they moved from one watchtower to another.**

1. How could you find out more about the Great Wall of China?
2. How else can people protect their homes and cities from invaders?
3. Pretend you are a laborer building the Great Wall. What do you think your life would be like? What kinds of equipment would you and the other workers use?
4. In New York City, the crowded theater district is often called the Great White Way. Why do you think it is called this name?
5. What other places in the world can you think of that have the word **great** in them?
6. Why are all these places called "great"?

One Step Further

Write a short report on the country of China. Find out where it is located, how big it is, the name and location of its capital city, and how many people live there. What kind of government does China have? What kinds of sports and entertainment are popular there? When you are done, draw a picture to illustrate one interesting fact from your report.

What is the metric system?

Today, most countries in the world use the metric system of measurement. In the 1790s, French scientists created this measurement system that was so easy to use it spread throughout most of the world. The metric system uses meters to measure length, grams to measure weight, and liters to measure amounts. In addition to the metric system, the United States still uses the standard English system of measurement, which includes inches, miles, ounces, and pounds.

1. How long has the metric system been in use?
2. How many centimeters are in one meter?
3. Which one is longer, a centimeter or an inch?
4. Look at some of the containers in your house. Which ones use the metric system? Which ones use the standard English system? Which ones use both?
5. Measure things in your house, such as the width of your TV screen or the length of your toothbrush, in both systems. What are the measurements of each object?
6. One metric liter of liquid is equal to a little more than four standard cups of liquid. About how many liters and cups of liquid did you drink today?

When was the wheel invented?

We don't know exactly when the wheel was invented, but we do know that people were using wheels to move things more than 5,000 years ago. Round logs were probably the first types of wheels. People placed the logs under big, heavy objects and moved the objects by pushing them over the logs. The first two-wheeled vehicle was probably a *chariot*, which is a cart pulled by a horse. This vehicle was followed by other two- and four-wheeled carts.

1. How do you think a wheelchair got its name?
2. Why do people use wheelbarrows? What does a wheelbarrow look like?
3. What is a pinwheel?
4. What does a wheelwright do? If you do not know, how could you find out?
5. On a separate piece of paper, make a list of as many things as you can think of that have wheels. How many did you write down?
6. Imagine that you have to move things without the help of wheels. How would you do this?

❓ What is historical fiction?

Historical fiction is a make-believe story that is based on actual events from history. This kind of story helps teach us what life was like during different time periods. A historical fiction story might be a make-believe tale about a Puritan family living in colonial America or a Native American family from the old Wild West.

1. What historical fiction stories have you read? When did these stories take place?

2. What kinds of things do children have today that children living in Plymouth Colony in 1620 may not have had?

3. If you were to create a historical fiction story, when and where would your story take place? How could you find out what life was like at that time?

4. What kinds of clothes would your historical fiction characters wear?

5. Pretend you are a child living in America during colonial times. On a separate piece of paper, write a journal entry about your life. What would you do each day?

6. If your future grandchildren were to create a historical fiction story about your life today, what kinds of things would you want them to write about?

What are cable cars?

Cable cars are special cars that are pulled by a moving cable. They are used to take people and supplies up and down hills and mountains that are too steep for cars, buses, or trucks to easily climb. They are also used to get people and things from one side of a deep canyon to another. The cable cars ride along cables that are made of steel ropes that are often twisted together to make them very strong.

1. What is the cable car being used for in the picture?
2. Have you ever seen or ridden in a cable car? When? Where was it?
3. Where might you find a lot of cable cars that take people up a mountain?
4. What would the trees, a river, and animals look like if you saw them from a cable car taking you across a deep canyon?
5. What do you think a cable railway is? Why would people build one?
6. Some sweaters are made with a special knitting design called a cable stitch. What do you think this looks like?

What are myths?

Myths are old fictional stories that explain why things are the way they are. Myths are not based on real facts or scientific study. Often myths include make-believe creatures or people who can perform superhuman feats. People of all cultures have myths that tell about things such as how the world began, how people were created, and how the sun and the moon got into the sky. A collection of several myths about one country or person put together in a book is called a *mythology*.

1. What myths have you heard or read? What were they about?
2. Which is your favorite myth? Why?
3. If you wanted to find a mythological explanation for why we have four seasons each year, where would you look?
4. Do you know any myths that have special wishes as the main idea of the story? If not, where could you find some?
5. If a person tells you that something sounds like a myth, what does he or she mean?
6. Be a mythologist. On a separate piece of paper, write your own myth to explain why we have day and night.

What is skywriting?

Skywriting is writing in the sky made by smoke trailing from a flying airplane. The large white fluffy letters made by the smoke spell out a word or short message. This smoke is created by mixing chlorine gas with a metal called titanium (ti-TAY-nee-um). A skywriting airplane has a special tank to carry this mixture. The pilot releases the smoke as he or she uses the plane like a pen and forms letters.

1. Have you ever seen skywriting? What was the message written in the sky?

2. Pretend you are a skywriting pilot. What message would you write?

3. On a separate piece of paper, draw a picture of you in your skywriting airplane. What message are you writing?

4. What do you think happens to the puffs of smoke a few minutes after they have been released from the plane?

5. What other ways do people display messages in the sky?

6. How many different words can you think of that begin with the word **sky**?

What is science fiction?

Science fiction is an imaginary story that predicts or tells what life may be like in the future. These predictions are based on what we now know about science and technology. They usually describe or explain some current or futuristic scientific experience. Science fiction stories include things such as robots, spaceships, and extraterrestrial (or alien) beings, as well as futuristic places, machines, food, and clothing.

1. What kinds of science fiction stories or space adventure books have you read?
2. Which science fiction stories are your favorites? What makes them so special?
3. If you could travel into the future, what would you take with you?

4. If aliens, or extraterrestrials, came to visit you on earth, what would you feed them? What would you show them? Where would you take them?

5. What do you think life would be like for us if we had robots in our homes? On a separate piece of paper, write a short story about how you would use robots to help you every day. Then draw a picture to go with your story.

6. Pretend you could travel into the future. Create a science fiction travel journal, complete with illustrations. What year would you travel to? Who would you visit? Would you go to any other planets? How would you get there from Earth? What will your life be like in this futuristic place?

One Step Further

Ask an adult to help you find materials around your house that you can use to create a futuristic city. What will your city's buildings look like? What kinds of transportation systems will you make for your city? How will you dress your people?

❓ What are pyramids?

More than 4,000 years ago, the pyramids were built as *tombs,* or burial chambers, for ancient Egyptian kings, known as *pharaohs.* It took many years to build these huge buildings, which were made of hundreds of heavy stone blocks. A team of workers tied these large stones to sleds and dragged them into place, one at a time. Ramps were used to get the stones to the upper levels of the tall pyramids. It took over two million stones to build the pharaoh Khufu's tomb, which is called the **Great Pyramid of Giza.** It is the biggest pyramid of all and one of the largest stone structures ever built! Inside this almost 500 feet tall pyramid, there are three chambers, or rooms. Khufu was buried in the largest chamber. Jewels, furniture, food, and hunting equipment filled the other two chambers.

1. Most pyramids are no longer standing, but pieces of them have been saved. Have you ever seen pyramid ruins or any of the treasures found inside them? Where would you go if you wanted to see these historical treasures?

2. Where did the large stones used for building pyramids come from? How could you find out?

3. In what shape were the pyramids built? What materials could you use to create a model of a pyramid?

4. Why do you think many of the pharaohs' tombs were broken into and robbed?

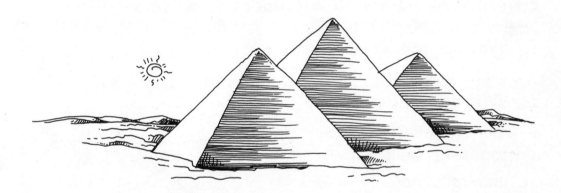

5. The sphinx is a large statue that was built to guard and protect the pyramid of the pharaoh Khafre, son of Khufu. What do you think the sphinx might look like? Explain your answer.

6. If you could create a magic time-traveling helmet to take you back in time, what would you use to make it? Where would you go? What time period would you visit?

Who was King Tut?

King Tut lived around 1350 B.C. and was the king, called a *pharoah*, of ancient Egypt. His full name was Tutankhamen. He became pharoah when he was 10 years old and ruled until he died at the age of 20. People became interested in King Tut when his secret underground tomb was discovered in 1922. His large rock tomb had several rooms that were filled with priceless treasures, including a gold mask that covered the head and shoulders of his body.

1. Why are some treasures called priceless?
2. Why do you think Tutankhamen's tomb was built underground?
3. For how many years did Tutankhamen rule as king of Egypt?

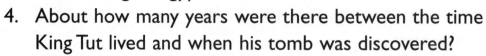

4. About how many years were there between the time King Tut lived and when his tomb was discovered?
5. King Tut's mummy was found in his tomb. What is a mummy?
6. How many smaller words can you make using the letters in the name **Tutankhamen**? See if you can make at least 10 words.

What are limericks?

Limericks are silly poems that have five lines. The first and second lines end with words that rhyme. The third and fourth lines end with different rhyming words. The fifth line usually ends with a surprising or funny statement. The last word of this line rhymes with the last word of the first two lines. Edward Lear, an Englishman who lived in the 1800s, is famous for making limericks popular. Here is a limerick from an anonymous, or unknown, author:

A tutor who taught on the flute
Tried to teach two tooters to toot.
Said the two to the tutor,
"Is it harder to toot, or
To tutor two tooters to toot?"

1. Have you read any limericks? What were they about?
2. Where can you find limericks to read?
3. Edward Lear died in 1888. How many years ago was that?
4. What other famous authors have written limericks for children? If you don't know, how could you find out?
5. Can you make up a tune to sing the limerick above?
6. Write your own limerick on a separate piece of paper. Can you use your name in your limerick?

How does a helicopter fly?

A helicopter can go straight up or down in the air because it has at least three horizontal rotor blades on top of it. As these rotor blades quickly twirl around in a circle, the air pressure under the blades pushes up and lifts the helicopter into the air. The pilot is able to move the helicopter forward or backward by changing the angle, or tilt, of the rotor blades. This is different from an airplane, which has wings, and propellers that whirl around in a vertical motion.

1. Why don't helicopters need to use a long runway to take off and land?

2. Helicopters are able to hover in the air. What does this mean?

3. What do you think a heliport is? Where might you find one?

4. Why are helicopters often used to transport badly injured people to a hospital?

5. If a helicopter can't land in the water, how would a person stranded at sea be put into a helicopter?

6. How might people travel 100 years from now? On a separate piece of paper, draw an illustration of a futuristic travel craft.

How does a compass work?

The needle in a compass is a magnet. It is fastened in the middle of the compass and can spin around. The needle always points north. The letters on the dial, or face, of the compass show all the directions: north, south, east, and west. People use a compass to help them find out in which direction they are traveling.

1. Look at the picture. Which direction is the compass needle pointing? What is the opposite of that direction? Which direction is the opposite of east?

2. Have you ever used a compass? What did you do with it?

3. How can you tell which direction is north on a map?

4. Who uses a compass as part of his or her job?

5. What is a weather vane? Why do some people have weather vanes on top of their roofs?

6. Why is it a good idea for a hiker to take along a compass when going on a long hike?

How can maps help us?

There are many different kinds of maps. Maps help us find the best route to go across town and help us discover how far it is between two states or two countries. They show what the world looks like, how deep the oceans are, and how tall certain mountains are. They can even tell us the population of a country or a state. Maps have special symbols that show us where things like schools, bridges, rivers, airports, and campgrounds are located. All maps have a legend, or key, that tells what each symbol stands for.

1. How many jobs can you name that have map reading as part of the job?
2. What is an atlas? Where could you find one?
3. On a separate piece of paper, draw a map of your state. Can you mark the location of your state capital and the city or town where you live?
4. What does it mean to "map out a project"?

5. What is the difference between a globe and a map? Why is it easier to use a map instead of a globe when you are traveling from one place to another?

6. Create a map, also called a *floor plan,* of your bedroom. Be sure to include everything in your room. How will you show your bed, your dresser, your toys, the window, and your closet?

One Step Further

Ask an adult to help you find and read a map of your neighborhood. Mark the exact location of your home on your map. Trace the shortest route you could walk from your home to places such as your school, your favorite playground or park, the public library, or the nearest grocery store. Then write directions from your home to a couple of these places. If you were walking from your house to the park, your directions might read like this: Go out the front door. Go down the steps to the sidewalk. Turn right and walk on the sidewalk to the end of the block. At the corner, turn left and carefully cross the street. Continue walking straight for two blocks. At the end of the second block, turn right. The park will be halfway down the block on the right side.

Why do beavers build dams?

A dam is a wall that holds back water. Beavers build dams in a narrow part of a stream or a lake to make a pond where they can build their homes. A family of beavers work together to make a dam. They pile up twigs, branches, and logs from bushes and trees. Then they scoop up mud and rocks with their flat tails to weigh down the branches and logs. The finished dam is about 3 or 4 feet high. The beavers build their home, called a *lodge*, out of branches and mud in the pond behind the dam. They enter the lodge through a tunnel that opens underwater.

1. Have you ever seen a dam built by beavers? What did it look like?
2. What do beavers look like?
3. How can a beaver's wide, flat tail and webbed feet help it build its dam?
4. Why do some people say the beaver is a great engineer?
5. On a separate piece of paper, draw a picture of a beaver family working hard to build a dam.
6. Make up a story about this beaver family. What adventures do they have as they go about their jobs?

What are tall tales?

Tall tales are make-believe stories about real people who have been made into superhuman heroes. These stories exaggerate and make up the heroes' good deeds and adventures. Some of the more famous tall tales are about **Paul Bunyan**, a giant lumberjack who, with the help of his blue ox, **Babe**, performed unbelievable feats, like digging the Grand Canyon and the Great Lakes! Pecos Bill, another tall-tale hero, was a skilled cowboy who could ride a cyclone.

1. What tall tales have you heard or read? What made them funny? What parts of the story were exaggerated or made up?

2. What does "stretching the truth" mean?

3. How do you think tall tales got their name?

4. How are these tall-tale heroes similar to modern superheroes such as Superman and Batman? How are they different?

5. If you were going to make up a tall tale, what superhuman feats would your main character perform?

6. Can you think of some funny illustrations to include in your tall tale? Draw them on a separate piece of paper.

Why do some people wear eyeglasses?

Some people wear eyeglasses to help them see more clearly. The most common eye problems people may have are being farsighted, nearsighted, or having an astigmatism (uh-STIG-muh-tiz-um). If a person is farsighted, it means he or she can only see things clearly that are far away. If a person is nearsighted, he or she can only see something clearly when it is very near. People who have an astigmatism have blurry or unclear vision all the time, no matter if things are near or far away.

1. Who do you know who wears eyeglasses? Why does that person have to wear glasses?
2. What are contact lenses? Do you know anyone who wears them?
3. Why isn't it nice to call someone who wears glasses "four eyes"?
4. Why do people wear sunglasses when they are outside?
5. Do you wear eyeglasses? On a separate piece of paper, draw a picture of yourself wearing glasses.
6. What is the name of the person who tests your eyesight, or tells you if you need to wear glasses?

Why does a mosquito bite itch?

When a mosquito pierces your skin, it sips some of your blood, which is a mosquito's food. This leaves a small bump on your skin. The itchy feeling around the bump is caused by your body's allergic reaction to the mosquito's saliva. If you are allergic to the mosquito's saliva, your body sends its germ fighters, called *antibodies,* to the area around the mosquito bump and makes your skin feel itchy. A mosquito doesn't really bite because it can't open its jaw. It stabs your skin using a long, thin tubelike part of its mouth. Most people call this mosquito piercing a bite.

1. Have you ever seen a mosquito land on your arm or leg? What happened to your skin after the mosquito flew away?
2. What would happen if a mosquito bit you and you were not allergic to the saliva?
3. Can you name some other insects that sting or pierce people's skin?
4. What sound do you think mosquitoes make?
5. How can you keep mosquitoes away from you?
6. Why do you think most people don't like mosquitoes?

What do archaeologists do?

Archaeologists are scientists who study old objects, called *artifacts*, like tools, bones, and buildings. The artifacts made and used by ancient people, such as jewelry, pots, dishes, coins, and statues, are clues that help archaeologists discover how people lived and even what language they spoke a long time ago. Archaeologists dig very carefully in the soil at an archaeological site and study the objects they find. These sites are located all over the world, where ancient people lived, worked, and played.

1. What are the people in the pictures doing?
2. Have you ever seen ancient artifacts in a museum? What did they look like? How did people use them?
3. Have you ever been to an archaeological site? When? Where was it? How could you find out where some sites are located?

4. If you were an archaeologist and you found these artifacts all together, what would they tell you about the ancient people?
   - animal bones
   - pieces of bowls
   - part of a jug
   - a sharp-edged stone tool
5. Where do you think archaeologists work when they aren't digging at an archaeological site?
6. What personal artifacts or clues would you want future archaeologists to find that tell about your life? Draw a picture of those artifacts on a separate piece of paper.

One Step Further
Ask an adult to help you be a detective and study or "read" clues from modern artifacts just like an archaeologist "reads" clues from ancient artifacts. For example, find a penny, a nickel, a dime, or a quarter. Use a magnifying glass to look very closely at this modern artifact. Make a list of everything you see, such as the date the coin was made, the person on the coin, and the language used on the coin. How many clues did you find?

What are homing pigeons?

Homing pigeons are types of pigeons that are born with a very special skill. These pigeons can find their way back home even if they are taken hundreds of miles away! Scientists aren't really sure how homing pigeons do this. People have been using homing pigeons, sometimes called *carrier pigeons*, for many years to transport messages from one place to another. A very long time ago, some homing pigeons were even used to deliver the mail!

1. Have you ever fed pigeons? What did you give them to eat?
2. What did the pigeons do and how did they sound?
3. How do homing pigeons hold the messages they deliver?

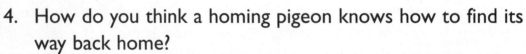

4. How do you think a homing pigeon knows how to find its way back home?
5. Where do you think pigeons go when there is a storm?
6. If you had a carrier pigeon, to whom would you send a message? What would your message say?

What are endangered animals?

There are many animals that are endangered. This means there are so few of these animals living today that they are in danger of disappearing from the earth forever, just like the dinosaurs. Sometimes animals become endangered when they lose their homes or food supply. Crocodiles, rhinoceroses, cheetahs, gray whales, and gorillas are some of the many endangered animals. For many years people have been hunting them for food or to sell their feathers, fur, or ivory tusks.

1. Look at the word **endanger**. What other, shorter word can you find inside of endanger? How does this other word help you to know what endanger means?
2. What very large African animal is endangered because some people hunt it for its ivory?
3. What are some other ways animals become endangered?
4. What do endangered animals need so they will grow in number?
5. Why are animals who live in national parks more protected than animals in the wild?
6. Can you create a poster that tells people how they can help endangered animals from becoming extinct?

Where do diamonds come from?

Diamonds are gems. Like other gems, such as rubies and sapphires, they are found in rocks and minerals that are located under the ground, as well as on the earth's surface. Once these rocks and minerals have been mined, or dug up, an expert carefully cuts and polishes the gemstone. Each type of gem is cut and polished in a special way to best show off its color and sparkle.

1. Have you seen jewelry made from cut and polished minerals? What gems were in the minerals?
2. Did you know you have a birthstone for your birthday month? Which gem is your special birthstone?
3. What color is the inside of a ruby grapefruit? How did it get its name?
4. Is a baseball diamond a gem?
5. What does it mean when a person says "You are a gem!"?
6. Why do you think the country of Ireland is sometimes called the Emerald Isle?

What is a wart?

A wart is a funny-looking hard bump on the skin. Warts are caused by really tiny germs, called *viruses*, that get into the cells of people's skin. Warts are *contagious*, which means they can spread from one part of your body to another part, or from one person to another person. Warts don't hurt unless they are on your feet, where they may rub against your shoes and make it painful to walk. Some warts will go away by themselves, but can also be removed by a doctor.

1. Does a wart on your hand hurt?
2. Why shouldn't you scratch or dig at a wart with your fingernails?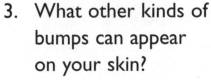
3. What other kinds of bumps can appear on your skin?
4. Some people say you can get warts from touching frogs. Do you think this is true? Why do people think this?
5. What does it mean when someone says "I love you, warts and all"?
6. Have you ever heard of a warthog? What is it? What do you think a warthog looks like?

Where do rocks come from?

Rocks come from the earth. In fact, the earth's crust is made up of different types of rocks. There are three main types of rocks. Igneous rocks come from very hot melted material, called *magma,* that is deep inside the earth. When volcanoes erupt, magma spills onto the earth's surface, and then it cools and hardens into lava rocks. Sedimentary rocks are formed from worn-away layers of older rocks, as well as from the remains of plants and animals. Fossils are found in sedimentary rocks. Metamorphic rocks are created out of other rocks that have been changed by heat or pressure. Marble is a metamorphic rock that comes from limestone.

1. Have you ever seen polished rocks or stones? How did they feel? What colors did you see in them?

2. What do we call a scientist who studies the earth, its history, and how rocks are formed? See if you can find a clue in the picture.

3. What is the name of a very old rock that has prints of animals or plants in it?

4. What is a very hot, melted igneous rock that is pushed up from under the ground when a volcano erupts? What color is it?

5. Marble is a hard, polished rock that is used to make statues, fancy floors, and tabletops. What kind of rock is it?

6. What is the most valuable rock that some people like to wear when it is cut and polished?

One Step Further

Go for a walk with an adult and look for different colored rocks to start a rock collection. Bring home your favorite ones. Clean your rocks with warm, soapy water and an old, wet toothbrush. Rinse them off and put them on newspaper to dry. Use an empty egg carton as your rock collection display box. Ask an adult to help you find a good book about rocks with lots of colored pictures. Try to find pictures of your rocks in the book. Label each rock with its name and where you found it.

Is a bald eagle really bald?

No, a bald eagle isn't bald. The adult bald eagle has short, smooth white feathers on its head. From a distance, these smooth white feathers make this bird look like it is bald, or has no feathers. Bald eagles weigh 8 to 13 pounds and are almost 3 feet long when grown. They have white tails and dark brown feathers on their wings and bodies. Bald eagles are strong hunting birds that live near water and eat mostly fish and dead animals. They are known to have very good eyesight and very powerful wings.

1. The bald eagle fishes from the air. How do you think it does this?
2. What coin has a picture of a bald eagle on it?
3. Why do you think the bald eagle is the national emblem or symbol of the United States?
4. What is the name of a hunting dog that rhymes with eagle? Can you name a bird whose name also rhymes with eagle?
5. What do you think it means to be "eagle-eyed"?
6. Pretend you are a meat-eating eagle. What would you eat and where would you live?

How do we catch a cold?

Colds are caused by viruses that are so tiny, you can't see them with your eyes. When someone with a cold sneezes or coughs, these small virus-filled droplets shoot out of his or her body and onto the objects around them. You may catch a cold if you come in contact with, or touch, these germs. Cold viruses go into your bloodstream, move around your body, and end up in your throat, nose, and chest. Germ fighters called *antibodies* fight cold germs and help a person get better.

1. Look at the children in the picture. What clues tell you that some of the children have caught a cold?
2. How did your eyes, nose, and throat feel the last time you had a cold?
3. How can you help yourself feel better when you have a cold?
4. Why do you sometimes get hot when you have a cold?
5. Do you catch a cold the same way you catch a ball?
6. Why do people tell others to cover their noses or mouths when they sneeze or cough?

Why do crocodiles look like they are smiling?

Crocodiles look like they are smiling because of the crooked shape of their jaws and their long rows of flashing teeth. But those powerful jaws and sharp teeth make this tough-skinned giant lizard one of the world's most dangerous animals. If the crocodile opens its smiling mouth, it is usually getting ready to gobble up some small animal for a snack.

1. The crocodile has a cousin who lives in the swamps and rivers of Florida. What is this cousin's name?

2. How many living and extinct members of the reptile family can you name?

3. Why are crocodiles in the water often mistaken for floating logs?

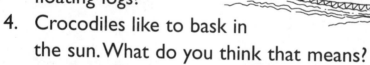

4. Crocodiles like to bask in the sun. What do you think that means?

5. Is a crocodile bird a bird that looks like a crocodile? What does a crocodile bird eat?

6. A person who cries "crocodile tears" is not really hurt or sad, but is crying pretend tears to get his or her own way. Make up a story about someone who is shedding "crocodile tears." Why is this person trying to get his or her own way?

Are owls really wise?

No, owls are not wise. They are no smarter than any other birds. An owl's appearance sometimes makes it look smarter. When an owl sits very still on its perch, it looks like it is deep in thought. Some people say the owl's big, round eyes make it appear like it is thinking very hard. These large, powerful eyes allow an owl to see easily at night when it hunts for food. An owl can even turn its head almost completely around and see what is above or behind it.

1. Have you ever heard an owl? What kind of sound does it make?
2. What other hunting birds have good eyesight for seeing and catching food?
3. Bats are other animals that sleep during the day and are active at night. Where do bats often sleep?
4. What does someone mean if he or she says "I don't give a hoot!"?
5. We say a person who is very smart is as wise as an owl. What kind of person do we compare to a lion, a mule, or a snail?
6. If you could turn your head upside down, what would you see above you? How would you look to others with your head like this?

Why are there seashells at the beach?

There are seashells at the beach because they have been washed up onto the sand by the ocean's waves. Usually shells are empty because the soft-bodied sea animals who live inside them have died. These shells are the homes or protective coverings for mollusks (MOL-usks). *Mollusk* is the name of an animal that has a hard shell on the outside to protect its soft body on the inside.

1. Have you ever looked for seashells at the beach? How many different kinds of seashells did you find? What colors and shapes were they?
2. What do people have that protects the inside of their bodies?
3. What other sea creatures have hard outer coverings?
4. What kinds of foods do you eat that have shells?
5. What word means the same thing as **sea**? What word sounds like **sea** but has a different meaning?
6. What does it mean when someone says "That person has really come out of his shell"?

What is Groundhog Day?

Groundhogs, or woodchucks, are small North American animals that hibernate, or sleep, throughout the cold winter each year. There is an old legend in Canada and the United States that says on February 2, Groundhog Day, the hibernating groundhog pops out of its warm underground hole. If the groundhog does not see its shadow, winter is over and the groundhog can come out of hibernation. But if the groundhog does see its shadow, there will be six more weeks of winter, and the groundhog burrows into its hole for another nap.

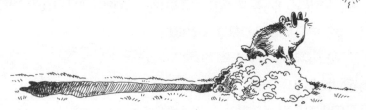

1. Why might the groundhog not be able to see its shadow?
2. Why do some animals hibernate during the cold winter?
3. Where do hibernating animals sleep?
4. If the groundhog comes out of its hole on February 2, sees its shadow, and goes back for a six-week nap, on what date will winter end?
5. If someone asks you "Have you been hibernating?" does that person think you've been sleeping all winter?
6. Pretend you are a hibernating animal. What would you do to get ready for your long winter's nap?

What is a tornado?

A tornado is a violent funnel-shaped windstorm. It forms when warm, wet air meets cool, dry air. As the hot air spins up from the earth, it twists around very fast in a circular shape. Tornadoes move very quickly over the land. A tornado can pick up a house and even cause it to break apart into pieces. It also can make cars fly through the air, pull trees up out of the ground, and lift water from a lake into the air.

1. Why are tornadoes called twisters?
2. What is the shape of a funnel?
3. A storm cellar is a deep underground shelter. Why do people go into a storm cellar when they learn that a tornado is coming?
4. What type of violent storm blows in from the ocean?
5. If you went on a tornado ride at an amusement park, what would the ride be like?
6. On a separate piece of paper, draw a picture of a tornado. Will your tornado be picking up a house, a car, or other objects?

What are hailstones?

Hailstones are clumps of ice that fall from the sky. Hail is formed when drops of water inside a storm cloud freeze into small pebbles of ice. These frozen raindrops fall to earth. Sometimes hailstones can pick up more freezing water on their way down and get bigger and bigger as they near the earth. Hail ranges from the size of a pea to the size of an orange. Some hailstones are big enough to make dents on cars or crack a car's windshield.

1. Why are clumps of hail called stones?
2. How could hail hurt people or animals?
3. How could hail damage crops of fruits and vegetables?
4. How are snow, sleet, and hail alike?
5. When you hail a taxicab, do you throw pieces of ice at the car?

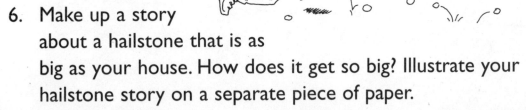

6. Make up a story about a hailstone that is as big as your house. How does it get so big? Illustrate your hailstone story on a separate piece of paper.

Where does the word *astronaut* come from?

In the old Greek language, *astro* meant "star" and *naut* meant "sailor." So the modern word *astronaut* really means "sailor of the stars." Today's astronauts are men or women trained to explore outer space. Astronauts use rockets to fly around the earth, to the moon, and to other planets in space.

1. What kind of trip is a nautical voyage? Do you take a plane, a boat, a train, or a car?
2. What do you think scientists called astronomers study?
3. What special clothing does an astronaut wear in outer space?
4. When a rocket is launched into space, there is a countdown till blast-off. What does this mean?
5. What kinds of foods do astronauts eat while in their rocket ships?
6. Make up a story starring yourself as an astronaut landing on a strange planet. What kind of imaginary space creatures will you meet?

What is the world's biggest bird?

The largest living bird in the world is the ostrich. It has a very long neck and strong long legs that help it move with great speed. A male ostrich can grow to be 7 or 8 feet tall and can weigh over 300 pounds. That's bigger than some of the largest humans. An ostrich can run as fast as a racehorse, but unlike most birds, it cannot fly, because it is too heavy and has short wings with small feathers.

1. What other animal has a very long neck and long legs?
2. What other birds cannot fly?
3. If an ostrich and a pigeon had a cross-country race, who do you think would win? Explain your answer.
4. On a separate piece of paper, can you draw a picture of this cross-country race?
5. How much more than you does a 300-pound ostrich weigh?
6. What does it mean when someone says "That person is just like an ostrich with his head in the sand"?

How can clouds help us predict the weather?

The shapes and sizes of the clouds help us predict weather. There are three main types of clouds. Fluffy clouds that look like cotton balls are cumulus clouds. When you see them, it will be a good weather day. The very high feathery clouds are cirrus clouds. They look like white streaks in the sky and often mean the weather is changing. Stratus clouds are low gray clouds that stretch for many miles. They usually mean that rain or snow is coming soon.

1. If the weather forecast says tomorrow will be a fair day, what does that mean?
2. Some people might say the day is partly sunny. Others might say it is partly cloudy. Do they both mean the same thing? Explain your answer.
3. What are the three main types of clouds?
4. Why do you think some people say cirrus clouds look like horses' tails?
5. Did you ever lie down in the grass and look up at the clouds? What shapes did you see in the clouds?
6. Keep a weather journal or diary for a week. Record how many days it is cloudy, sunny, wet, or dry.

Why do our stomachs growl when we are hungry?

If you haven't eaten in a long time, your empty stomach may make a loud growling noise. Scientists call this noise borborygmus (bor-buh-RIG-mus.) Your stomach naturally makes gurgling, bubbling noises as it works to digest your food. When your stomach is empty, these noises are louder because only air, not food, is being moved around your stomach. Food will help!

1. When was the last time you heard your stomach growl? How did it sound? How did it feel?

2. What do you think is happening in the picture?

3. If you hear your stomach rumbling, what can you do to stop the noise?

4. Ask a friend or a family member if you can put your ear on his or her stomach. What do you hear? Can you feel anything?

5. On a separate piece of paper, can you draw a picture of yourself when your stomach is growling?

6. Make up a song about a grumbling hungry tummy that is searching for food. What other words could you use in your song that rhyme with **grumbling** and **tummy**?

Answers

PAGE 5

1. Look in some books about medieval times, or go to a museum or art gallery that has displays of suits of armor and information about the Middle Ages.
2. He would be 21 years old.
3. Sample answers: Stories about King Arthur and the Knights of the Round Table, or Don Quixote.
4. Answers will vary.
5. Sample answer: Bendable cardboard or tinfoil could be wrapped around your arms, legs, and body.
6. Answers will vary.

PAGE 6

1. Answers will vary.
2. To protect them from enemy invasion.
3. Sample answers: They used simple hand tools, ropes, lifting gear, or machinery such as pulleys to raise heavy materials to a higher level.
4–6. Answers will vary.

PAGE 7

1–2. Answers will vary.
3. You could find out about the International Flag Code of Signals in books about flags.
4. A color guard is made up of several people who carry or escort the colors, or flags, in a parade. The flags are usually the national flag and the state flag, and the flag of the organization sponsoring the parade.
5. "Flag down that car" means to signal or wave your arms back and forth to try and stop an approaching car.
6. Answers will vary.

PAGES 8–9

1. Sample answers: Your heart might beat faster when you are jumping rope, swimming very fast, or when you are very excited or scared.
2. Sample answer: You can put two of your fingers on the inside of your friend's wrist to feel his or her pulse. Count the number of beats in one minute.
3. Put your ear on your friend's chest to hear his or her heartbeat.
4. Nurses and doctors use a stethoscope to listen to your heartbeat.
5. This means you are special to that person and the person's heart beats faster just thinking about you.

6. Answers will vary.

PAGES 10–11

1. Biographies for readers of all ages can be found in school or public libraries, in bookstores, and in some homes.
2. Answers will vary.
3. During the Civil War.
4. Answers will vary.
5. Sample answers: In your autobiography, you might include the date of your birth, the first words you said, when you first started to walk, when you first learned how to ride a bike, when you first started school, the members of your family, any pets you have, and your favorite toys.
6. Answers will vary.

PAGE 12

1. A canceled stamp is a stamp that has been sent through the mail and has been canceled, or marked, by the post office with ink. You cannot use a canceled stamp again.
2. Postcard stamps cost less than stamps used for a letter because the postcard weighs less than a letter in an envelope.
3–5. Answers will vary.
6. Mail is weighed and specific stamps are placed on the mail according to its weight. There is a special scale that tells people how many stamps are needed.

PAGE 13

1. Answers will vary.
2. Sample answers: Information about the first moon explorers and their discoveries can be found in libraries, bookstores, and on the Internet.
3. Answers will vary.
4. Sample answers: To become an explorer, you would need to be healthy, strong, brave, ready to take risks, and able to read a compass.
5. A surgeon operates on a particular area of the body to see what the problem might be in order to best treat a sick patient.
6. Answers will vary.

PAGES 14–15

1. Sample answers: Flatbed trucks, moving vans, refrigerator trucks, lumber trucks, and oil trucks.
2. Answers will vary.
3. A truck farmer grows fruits and vegetables on his farm and travels

around to different towns, cities, and farmers' markets to sell his goods from his truck.
4. A hand truck is a small kind of wheelbarrow with an open frame. It is used to carry crates, trunks, or small pieces of furniture.
5. This means to walk or stroll in a leisurely, carefree manner.
6. Because they are constantly driving on the road, "battling" the traffic as they deliver their cargo from one place to another, just as ancient knights used to battle.

PAGE 16

1. A stopwatch and a thermometer.
2. Sample answers: A ruler or a yardstick.
3. An hour and a half equals 90 minutes.
4. Sample answers: A stopwatch, a clock, an hourglass, a sundial, or a calendar.
5. Sample answers: Weight, height, and temperature.
6. Sample answers: Doctors use a thermometer to measure one's temperature, farmers use scales to measure the weight of their food crop, truck drivers use odometers to measure how far they have traveled, and airline pilots and ship captains use maps and charts to measure the distance they need to travel from one place to another.

PAGE 17

1. They are using parts of their bodies such as a foot, a hand span, and an elbow to fingertip length.
2. The measurements would be different because an adult and a young child don't have the same size feet.
3. Sample answers: You could use your foot, the number of paces or steps taken, or your hand spans to measure your bedroom.
4–6. Answers will vary.

PAGES 18–19

1. You could go to a library, a bookstore, or a museum to find more about the Great Wall of China.
2. Sample answers: Fences, gates, alarm systems, moats, and security people.
3. Answers will vary.
4. It has this name because there are so many lights on the theater marquees that at night it looks like

streets of bright, shiny lights.

5. Sample answers: Great Britain, the Great Lakes, Great Salt Lake, the Great Plains, the Great Barrier Reef, or the Great Divide (also called the Continental Divide).

6. Sample answer: These places are called "great" because they are large in size.

PAGE 20
1. Approximately 207 years.
2. There are 100 centimeters in one meter.
3. The inch is longer.
4–6. Answers will vary.

PAGE 21
1. Because wheels were attached to a chair to move a person who couldn't walk.
2. People use wheelbarrows to carry small, heavy loads from one place to another. A wheelbarrow has one front wheel, a shallow, open boxlike area for carrying a load, two legs in the back so the wheelbarrow will stand, and two handles so it can be moved by wheeling it forward.
3. A pinwheel is a small hand-held wheel on a stick with strips of paper that are pinned to the stick so they can revolve, or rotate, in the wind.
4. A wheelwright is a person who repairs wheels and wheeled vehicles. To find out, you could look in a dictionary.
5. Sample answers: A trike, bike, wagon, cart, car, truck, baby stroller and carriage, wheelbarrow, and a wheelchair.
6. Answers will vary.

PAGE 22
1. Answers will vary.
2. Sample answers: Children today must have their basic needs met to survive, such as food, clothing, and a place to live. They also need things to play with and some sort of education. Children today have more sophisticated toys, more choices for food and clothes, movies, videos, CDs, television, and more choices of books than children of the past.
3. Sample answers: Facts about life in the past can be found in museums, bookstores, and libraries.
4–6. Answers will vary.

PAGE 23
1. The cable car in the picture is being used to carry people across a canyon.
2. Answers will vary.
3. Sample answer: At a ski resort.
4. Answers will vary.
5. A cable railway is a railway car that moves a lot of people or cargo up or down a steep hill or mountain, or across a deep canyon.
6. Sample answer: A knitted cable stitch has a twisted look, and the design is

repeated over and over again.

PAGE 24
1–2. Answers will vary.
3. Sample answers: In a book of myths or an encyclopedia.
4. Answer will vary. Child could find such a myth in a mythology book.
5. He or she means that the statement or story is probably imaginary and not based on actual facts.
6. Answers will vary.

PAGE 25
1–3. Answers will vary.
4. Sample answer: The puffs of smoke begin to move apart and eventually disappear as the wind and air currents move through them.
5. Sample answers: Messages can be seen trailing on banners behind small airplanes, and on the undersides of blimps.
6. Sample answers: Skycap, skylark, skylight, skyline, skyscraper, skyward, and skyways.

PAGES 26–27
1–6. Answers will vary.

PAGES 28–29
1. Sample answers: You can find pieces of some pyramids and the treasures found inside them in many museums around the world.
2. The large stone blocks used for the pyramids came from local quarries, places where stone is dug out of the earth. You can find out more about the pyramids and how they were built from books and videotapes about them.
3. They were built in the shape of large triangles. Rest of answer will vary.
4. Many of the pharaohs' tombs were broken into and robbed because they contained so many valuable or expensive jewels, coins, furniture, and hunting equipment.
5–6. Answers will vary.

PAGE 30
1. *Priceless* means something is beyond a dollar value or price, usually because it is so rare.
2. Tutankhamen was buried in a secret underground rock tomb to keep robbers from stealing all the gold and treasures that were buried with him.
3. Tutankhamen ruled for 10 years.
4. There were about 3,300 years between the time that Tutankhamen lived and when his tomb was found.
5. A mummy is a preserved dead body that has not decayed. To do this, the ancient Egyptians removed the internal organs and covered the body with salt until it dried out. Linen was then stuffed inside it, and the entire body

was tightly wrapped with hundreds of strips of linen bandages.
6. Sample answers: Amen, Ann, Anna, ant, at, ma, man, mat, men, name, Nan, Nat, Nate, net, nut, tan, tank, taut, ten, tent.

PAGE 31
1. Answers will vary.
2. Sample answers: In poetry books found at home, in bookstores, and in libraries.
3. Edward Lear died 109 years ago.
4. Sample answers: Rudyard Kipling, Ogden Nash, John Ciardi, Arnold Lobel, and William Jay Smith. You could find out in a library.
5–6. Answers will vary.

PAGE 32
1. Because they can go straight up or down when they take off or land.
2. To hover in the air means to stay suspended in one place in the air.
3. A heliport is a space where helicopters can take off and land, such as a small field or even the flat roof of a building.
4. Because they can get to and from the accident site and the hospital quicker than an automobile, which may get stuck in traffic.
5. A stretcher or life ring is lowered to the person being rescued as the helicopter hovers in one place. Sometimes a helicopter crew member wearing a safety harness is lowered down to help the person being rescued.
6. Answers will vary.

PAGE 33
1. The compass needle is pointing north. The opposite direction is south. West is opposite east.
2. Answers will vary.
3. North is almost always indicated, or shown, on a map by an arrow that is labeled *N*.
4. Airplane pilots, boat and ship captains, and leaders of climbing or hiking expeditions use a compass as part of their job.
5. A weather vane tells from which direction the wind is blowing. Some people have weather vanes on the tops of their roofs so they can easily see which way the wind is blowing.
6. Sample answer: Hikers can use a compass to note the direction they are going and the direction from which they have come.

PAGES 34–35
1. Sample answers: Airplane pilots, boat and ship captains, fire fighters, travel agents, police officers, and truck drivers.

2. An atlas is a book containing a collection of different kinds of maps. An atlas can be found in libraries, schools, bookstores, and in some homes.
3. Answers will vary.
4. To map out a project means to plan in detail how you are going to do it from beginning to end.
5. A map is a detailed representation of the earth on a flat surface. It can be folded to show just the area you need to see as you are traveling. A globe is a ball or sphere that is shaped just like the earth and shows all the land and water. It doesn't show small areas in detail and it is more difficult to carry around.
6. Answers will vary.

PAGE 36
1. Answers will vary.
2. A beaver is a large rodent with a broad, flat tail, webbed hind feet, very strong, sharp teeth, and soft brown fur.
3. The beaver's tail acts like a boat rudder and helps it move in the right direction as it carries building materials through the water to its dam. The webbed hind feet act like paddles and help it move quickly through the water.
4. Because beavers change the land around them to build homes by cutting down trees and building dams that help to form ponds.
5–6. Answers will vary.

PAGE 37
1. Answers will vary.
2. It means to exaggerate or add to a real story to make it funnier or more amazing.
3. Tall tales got their name from the fact that they brag, stretch the truth, or exaggerate realistic happenings to make them bigger-than-life or "tall" tales.
4–6. Answers will vary.

PAGE 38
1. Answers will vary.
2. Contact lenses are very thin, small lenses that correct vision. They are made of plastic or glass and are carefully placed in the natural fluid over the eye's cornea (the outer covering of the eye). Rest of answer will vary.
3. To call someone "four eyes" can hurt a person's feelings. People can't help the fact that they need to wear glasses to see things clearly.
4. Sunglasses have special tinted lenses that protect the eyes from the harmful glare and rays of the sun.
5. Answers will vary.

6. An optometrist is trained to examine eyes and prescribe corrective glasses or lenses. An ophthalmologist is trained to deal with the structure, functions, and diseases of the eyes.

PAGE 39
1. Sample answer: When a mosquito bites, it might feel itchy if you are allergic to the mosquito's saliva. The bite will become a raised bump on your skin.
2. No bumps or welts would form on your skin.
3. Other insects that sting or pierce people's skin are bees, hornets, wasps, and some spiders.
4. Mosquitoes make a soft buzzing or humming sound, which is caused by the beating of their wings.
5. Sample answers: By using mosquito repellent cream, citronella candles, mosquito netting, screens on windows and open doors, and a fly swatter.
6. Sample answers: People dislike mosquitoes because they carry diseases and they bite.

PAGES 40–41
1. The people in the pictures have found a dinosaur skull and a pot at archaeological sites. One person is using a magnifying glass to look at the skull.
2. Answers will vary.
3. You can find out about archaeological sites through books, videos, and films.
4. Sample answer: The artifacts would probably tell you that these ancient people used a sharp-edged stone tool to cut the animal meat for food, which was served in bowls with jugs of liquid to drink.
5. Archaeologists work in museums or universities doing research, writing about their findings, and teaching others.
6. Answers will vary.

PAGE 42
1. Answers will vary.
2. Sample answer: Pigeons usually flock, or gather around, if you throw bread crumbs or birdseed on the ground. They try to push each other out of the way to get to the food. Pigeons make a soft cooing sound.
3. Carrier pigeons carry messages strapped to their legs or backs. They don't hold the messages in their beaks!
4. Scientists aren't sure how pigeons do this, especially if they are many miles away from their homes.
5. In stormy weather, pigeons find shelter in their nests in trees, in the roofs of buildings or barns, or on the undersides of bridges.
6. Answers will vary.

PAGE 43
1. *Danger.* This word helps you to know the meaning of *endanger* because to be in danger means something is being threatened, hurt, or lost.
2. The elephant.
3. Animals can become endangered when they are hunted and sold to wildlife game parks and to research labs for testing of products.
4. Endangered animals need to be protected and given space to live where they can hunt for their food and raise their young.
5. National parks provide a lot of land, space, and protection for animals so they can live without being hunted and without their food supply being destroyed. Laws protect all the land and the animals and plants that live and grow in national parks.
6. Answers will vary.

PAGE 44
1. Sample answers: White or yellow diamonds, red rubies, green emeralds, different colors of topaz, purple amethyst, or blue-green turquoise.
2. You can often find your birthstone by looking in a date book or a dictionary.
3. Red. The ruby-red grapefruit is named after a ruby because its juicy fruit is red in color like a ruby.
4. No! A baseball diamond is the infield, which is in the shape of a diamond.
5. It means you are a very special, precious person.
6. Ireland is sometimes called the Emerald Isle because it has so many green fields the color of an emerald.

PAGE 45
1. No.
2. When you irritate or pick at a wart, it may bleed. The virus in the irritated wart may spread to other skin cells and cause more warts to grow.
3. Other bumps that can appear on the skin are pimples, moles, boils, or cysts.
4. You can't get warts from touching a frog. This is a superstition that isn't true. The frog's bumpy skin looks like it is covered with warts, but they aren't warts at all!
5. Usually it means the person is still lovable no matter what he or she looks or acts like.
6. A warthog is a wild African hog. The males have cone-shaped pairs of warts or bumps on their cheeks between their eyes and their tusks.

PAGES 46–47
1. Answers will vary.
2. A geologist studies rocks.
3. A sedimentary rock contains fossils.
4. This is lava, which is a dark color, usually black.

5. Marble is a metamorphic rock formed from limestone.
6. A diamond is the most valuable rock.

PAGE 48

1. It has very sharp eyesight that lets it see fish swimming under the water. When the eagle sees a fish, it swoops down with its strong wings to grab the fish for dinner.
2. The bald eagle is pictured on the quarter.
3. Because it represents power, keen vision, and strength.
4. Beagle; seagull.
5. To be eagle-eyed means one has strong, clear vision or eyesight.
6. Answers will vary.

PAGE 49

1. The children in the picture are sneezing and coughing without covering their mouths.
2. Sample answers: Your eyes may have been watering, you probably had a stuffy nose, and your throat may have felt scratchy and sore.
3. Sample answers: Bed rest, drinking lots of fluids, and perhaps taking cough medicine will help you feel better.
4. You sometimes get hot when you have a cold because the virus causes a fever, which is an abnormal rise in your body temperature.
5. No. You catch a cold from cold viruses or germs.
6. To keep the cold germs from getting into the air and reaching other people and objects.

PAGE 50

1. Alligator.
2. Sample answers: Living reptiles include snakes, lizards, and turtles. Dinosaurs are extinct reptiles.
3. The crocodile's thick, horny skin with its scales and plates is dark colored. When the crocodile is very still in the water, all you can see is the top part of its back and head, which makes it look like a dark, bumpy log floating in the water.
4. To warm oneself in the heat of the sunshine.
5. A crocodile bird is an African bird that likes to eat the parasites that live on the back of a crocodile. This bird doesn't look like a crocodile, it just likes to sit on a crocodile's back to eat dinner!
6. Answers will vary.

PAGE 51

1. An owl makes a very distinctive sound: "Whoo, whoo, whoo."
2. Vultures, hawks, and eagles have good eyesight for seeing and catching small animals and fish to eat.

3. Bats sleep during the day and can be seen hanging upside down from the roof of a cave or the rafters of a barn.
4. This usually means the person doesn't care about something.
5. People sometimes use similes to compare others to animals, such as "that person is as brave or courageous as a lion," or "that person is as stubborn as a mule," or "that person is as slow as a snail."
6. Answers will vary.

PAGE 52

1. Answers will vary.
2. People have a skeleton that protects the inside of their bodies.
3. Lobsters and crabs have hard outer coverings, or shells, to protect their bodies.
4. Sample answers: Eggs, coconuts, walnuts, peanuts, crabs, lobsters, clams, and snails all have hard shells.
5. *Ocean* means the same thing as *sea*. *See* is the homonym for *sea*: It sounds the same but is spelled differently and has a different meaning.
6. This means the person no longer seems to be shy and is more comfortable talking and playing with others.

PAGE 53

1. The groundhog wouldn't be able to see its shadow on a cloudy, foggy, or rainy day because the sun wouldn't be shining.
2. They hibernate because they can't move around easily and find food during the cold winter.
3. They hibernate inside deep caves or holes in the ground.
4. Six weeks, or 42 days, from February 2 will be March 16 if February has 28 days, and March 15 if it is a leap year and February has 29 days.
5. No! It means the person hasn't seen you in a very long time.
6. Answers will vary.

PAGE 54

1. Because the wind moves or spins around in a twisting, circular motion.
2. Cone shaped, like an ice-cream cone.
3. To stay safe underground away from the windstorm.
4. A hurricane or a typhoon.
5–6. Answers will vary.

PAGE 55

1. Because they are as hard as rocks.
2. As it falls to the earth hail can hit them.
3. By bruising the skin or outer covering and breaking the plants or branches as it falls to the earth.
4. They are forms of frozen rain.
5. No! Hail also means to wave. To hail a

cab means you are waving your arm at the cab to signal it to stop and take you where you need to go.
6. Answers will vary.

PAGE 56

1. It is a trip on a boat.
2. The position, measurements, and appearances of the stars and planets.
3. A special space suit created to keep his or her body temperature normal and to protect the astronaut while in space.
4. The hours, minutes, and seconds are counted down or backward until zero is reached and it is time for blast-off.
5. All sorts of freeze-dried, compressed food.
6. Answers will vary.

PAGE 57

1. A giraffe.
2. The penguin, emu, and rhea are all flightless birds.
3. Sample answer: The pigeon would probably win because it can fly faster than an ostrich can run.
4–5. Answers will vary.
6. This means that the person doesn't want to see or know about the things that are happening around him or her, especially if those things are troublesome.

PAGE 58

1. It means that the sun will be shining and there will not be any rain, sleet, hail, or snow.
2. A day that is partly sunny or partly cloudy means the same thing, as there are some clouds that sometimes block out the sun for a few minutes as they drift in the sky.
3. Cumulus, cirrus, and stratus.
4. This is because cirrus clouds are white streaks in the sky that often have a slight curve to them and look very much like the tail of a horse.
5–6. Answers will vary.

PAGE 59

1. Answers will vary.
2. The children in the picture are laughing because one of their stomachs is making a funny-sounding growling noise.
3. You can eat somthing, that will stop the growling stomach sound.
4. Sample answer: You will hear a grumbling sound and may even feel a slight vibration or movement of the stomach muscles.
5–6. Answers will vary.

Other

books that will help develop your child's gifts and talents

Workbooks:
- Reading (4–6) $4.95
- Math (4–6) $4.95
- Language Arts (4–6) $4.95
- Puzzles & Games for Reading and Math (4–6) $3.95
- Puzzles & Games for Reading and Math Book Two (4–6) $4.95
- Puzzles & Games for Critical and Creative Thinking (4–6) $4.95
- Reading Book Two (4–6) $4.95
- Math Book Two (4–6) $4.95
- Phonics (4–6) $4.95
- Phonics Puzzles & Games (4–6) $4.95
- Math Puzzles & Games (4–6) $4.95
- Reading Puzzles & Games (4–6) $4.95
- Math (6–8) $3.95
- Language Arts (6–8) $4.95
- Puzzles & Games for Reading and Math (6–8) $3.95
- Puzzles & Games for Critical and Creative Thinking (6–8) $3.95
- Puzzles & Games for Reading and Math, Book Two (6–8) $3.95
- Phonics (6–8) $4.95
- Reading Comprehension (6–8) $4.95

Reference Workbooks:
- Word Book (4–6) $3.95
- Almanac (6–8) $3.95
- Atlas (6–8) $3.95
- Dictionary (6–8) $3.95

Story Starters:
- My First Stories (6–8) $3.95
- Stories About Me (6–8) $3.95
- Stories About Animals (6–8) $4.95

Question & Answer Books:
- The Gifted & Talented® Question & Answer Book for Ages 4–6 $5.95
- The Gifted & Talented® Question & Answer Book for Ages 6–8 $5.95
- Gifted & Talented® More Questions & Answers for Ages 4–6 $5.95
- Gifted & Talented® More Questions & Answers for Ages 6–8 $5.95

Drawing Books:
- Learn to Draw (6 and up) $5.95

Readers:
- Double the Trouble (6–8) $7.95
- Time for Bed (6–8) $7.95

For Parents:
- How to Develop Your Child's Gifts and Talents During the Elementary Years $11.95
- How to Develop Your Child's Gifts and Talents in Math $15.00
- How to Develop Your Child's Gifts and Talents in Reading $15.00
- How to Develop Your Child's Gifts and Talents in Vocabulary $15.00

Available where good books are sold! **or** *Send a check or money order, plus shipping charges, to:*

Handy Worksheet

Department TC
Lowell House
2020 Avenue of The Stars, Suite 300
Los Angeles, CA 90067

For special or bulk sales, call (800) 552-7551, EXT 30
Note: Minimum order of three titles. **On a separate piece of paper,** please specify exact titles and ages and include a breakdown of costs, as follows:

(# of books) ____ x $3.95 = ____			(Subtotal)		=	____
(# of books) ____ x $4.95 = ____			California residents			
(# of books) ____ x $5.95 = ____			add 8.25% sales tax		=	____
(# of books) ____ x $7.95 = ____			Shipping charges			
(# of books) ____ x $11.95 = ____			(# of books) ____ x $1.00/ book		=	____
(# of books) ____ x $15.00 = ____			**Total cost**		=	____